Stress Less, Enjoy More

Practical and Scriptural Stress Management Techniques to Tame Your Stress and Experience Peace

(Prepare for Excellence Series)

By

Sherry M. Carroll

Published by Truth Family Resources LLC

Stress Less, Enjoy More
http://www.PrepareForExcellence.com

Thank you for purchasing this book.
As a thank you, I want to give you a free report
called: ***Secrets of Motivated People***
Follow this link for some great information and
to receive this free resource:
http://prepareforexcellence.com/stress-download/
Thanks again!

ISBN: 978-0692421307

Disclaimer

While all attempts have been made to provide effective, verifiable information in this Book, neither the author nor publisher assumes any responsibility for errors, inaccuracies, or omissions. This publication is designed to provide accurate and authoritative information in regard to the subject matter covered. However, it is not a source of business, financial, or medical information and should not be regarded as such.

Quoted scripture is from the New International Version (NIV), unless otherwise noted.

TABLE OF CONTENTS

INTRODUCTION

Everywhere you go, you find people talking about how stressed they are. You would have a hard time locating anyone who does not have stress in their life.

If you go to the deepest part of the jungle and find a previously undiscovered tribe – people who do not have watches or technology – you might think they would have no stress. After all, without the pressure of modern life, it would be so much easier . . . right? Wrong! They would still have stress. There would be illnesses, accidents, pressure to hunt and gather food, natural disasters, relationship issues with their fellow tribesmen, worry for their children or elderly parents, etc.

The fact is that ALL people have stress in their lives: rich people and poor people, beautiful people and plain people, old people and young people, well-educated people and school drop-outs, spiritual people and non-believers. Money, power, education, spirituality or good looks – none of these shield people from stress.

Stress is a natural part of life, and not all stress is bad.

All animals have a stress response. The nerve chemicals and hormones which are released during stressful times prepare the animal to face a threat or to flee to safety.

When you face a dangerous situation, your pulse quickens, you breathe faster, your muscles tense, and your brain uses more oxygen and increases activity. These are all functions focused on survival. The problems come when the effects of stress continue, and that is the focus of this book.

Over 50% of stressed out people say they experience fatigue and irritability due to stressful issues. Chronic stress can lead to more serious issues including anxiety, panic attacks, and depression.

Left unchecked, the effects of stress can cause physical, emotional, and behavioral disorders which affect health, vitality, and peace-of-mind, as well as personal and professional relationships.

Stress is such a huge issue that April has been declared "Stress Awareness Month."

If you regularly feel stressed out, then it is time to take action. In the following chapters, you will learn some of the common causes of stress, identify the stressors in your life, and discover some of your behaviors which are keeping stress alive. Then, once identified, you will learn to deal with and minimize the effects of stress.

This book will include many practical tools you can use to help manage your stress. These tools/techniques are available to everyone. In addition, we will look at some biblical tools – some spiritual resources – which are only available to those who are Christians, those who follow Jesus as their Savior.

Thank you for reading this book; I hope you gain many insights that will help you improve your own response to stress so that you can Stress Less and Enjoy More!

Sherry M. Carroll

Stress is an important dragon to slay – or at least tame – in your life.
— Marilu Henner

WHAT IS STRESS?

The dictionary defines stress as:

---

a condition of extreme difficulty, pressure, or strain;

a condition of psychological strain occurring in people and animals, usually in response to adverse events and capable of causing symptoms and signs such as increased blood pressure, insomnia, and irritability;

physical, mental, or emotional strain or tension

Synonyms for stress include: burden, exertion, struggle, strain, pressure, tension, worry, anxiety, trouble, or difficulty.

Types of Stress

There are several types of stress:

- Positive stress – also called eustress; this is the stress that helps individuals function better, stay alive and cope

- Routine stress – that related to the pressures of work, family and other daily responsibilities

- Acute stress - stress brought about by a sudden negative change, such as losing a job, divorce, or illness

- Traumatic stress – that experienced in an event like a major accident, war, assault, or a natural disaster where one may be seriously hurt or in danger of being killed

Stress is often caused by some type of change. Even positive changes – such as getting married, having a baby, or winning a contest – can be stressful. The body responds to each type of stress, positive or negative, in similar ways.

Stress vs. Stressors

There is an important difference between stress and stressors. Stress is the way you <u>feel or the effects</u> on your life when under pressure. A stressor is the <u>factor or issue</u> in your life that causes the pressure.

You may have no control over the stressors in your life. There is nothing you can do about the traffic on your commute to work or the rude person who cuts in line in front of you at the grocery store or the noise of the construction right outside your work window. Therefore, the main focus of this book is stress and its effects on your life.

Effects of Stress

The effects of stress will not be the same for every individual. Just as some people have a higher pain tolerance, some people will not be as susceptible to the effects of stress as others. Different people will respond to stress in different ways. For example, some people experience mainly digestive symptoms, while others may have headaches, sleeplessness, depressed mood, anger, or irritability.

Those same nerve chemicals which are life-saving in short bursts become a problem with continued or chronic stress. A person's immunity is lowered, and various biological systems stop working normally.

This following diagram illustrates some of the physical effects of stress:

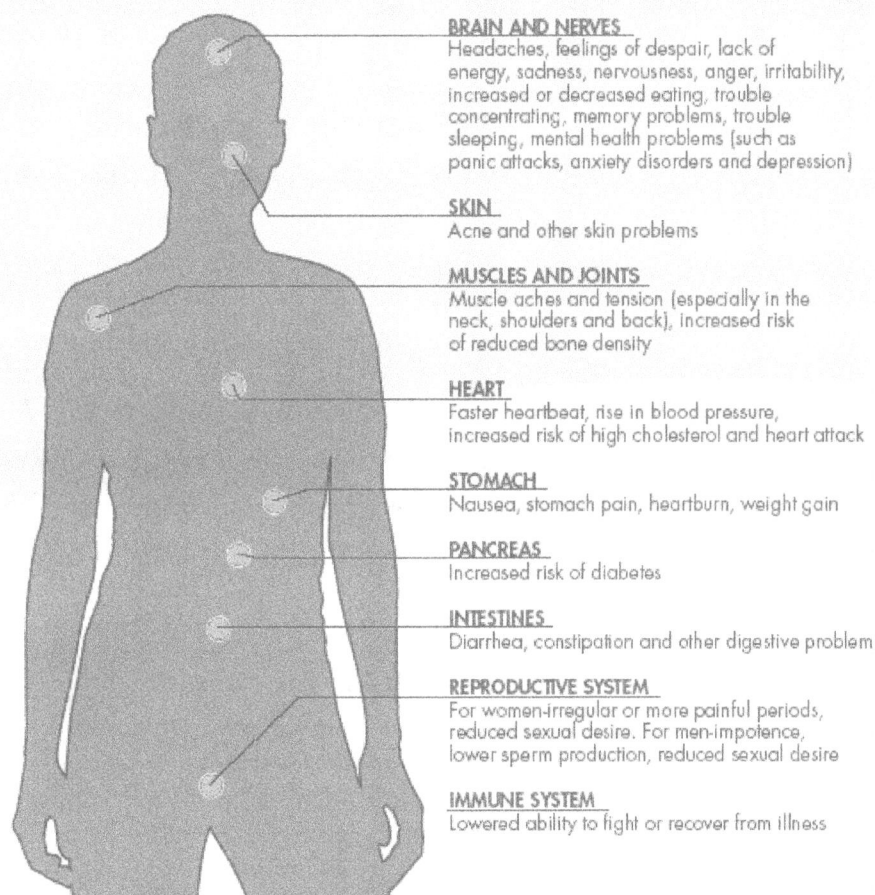

BRAIN AND NERVES
Headaches, feelings of despair, lack of energy, sadness, nervousness, anger, irritability, increased or decreased eating, trouble concentrating, memory problems, trouble sleeping, mental health problems (such as panic attacks, anxiety disorders and depression)

SKIN
Acne and other skin problems

MUSCLES AND JOINTS
Muscle aches and tension (especially in the neck, shoulders and back), increased risk of reduced bone density

HEART
Faster heartbeat, rise in blood pressure, increased risk of high cholesterol and heart attack

STOMACH
Nausea, stomach pain, heartburn, weight gain

PANCREAS
Increased risk of diabetes

INTESTINES
Diarrhea, constipation and other digestive problem

REPRODUCTIVE SYSTEM
For women-irregular or more painful periods, reduced sexual desire. For men-impotence, lower sperm production, reduced sexual desire

IMMUNE SYSTEM
Lowered ability to fight or recover from illness

If you are already dealing with a chronic disease, stress can make your symptoms worse. Your immune system is not in tip top shape, and this makes it very easy for you to get sick more often.

Stress is linked to diseases of the heart including; high blood pressure, abnormal heartbeats, blood clots, heart failure, hardening of the arteries, and can also lead to you having a major heart attack or stroke.

Stress affects your muscles, and you may notice that you suddenly suffer more joint pain and muscle spasms. The neck, shoulders and lower back area are most often affected. If you have rheumatoid arthritis, stress can make this condition worse.

If you suffer from any type of stomach issue including ulcers, irritable bowel syndrome or digestive issues, all of these can be made worse when stress enters your life.

Skin conditions in teens and young adults are often more pronounced when these individuals are dealing with stressful situations.

Physical effects to the body are not the only results of stress. Your mind, behavior, and emotions are also affected. The following is a graphic illustrating some of the effects of stress on your whole life: body, mind, behavior, and emotions:

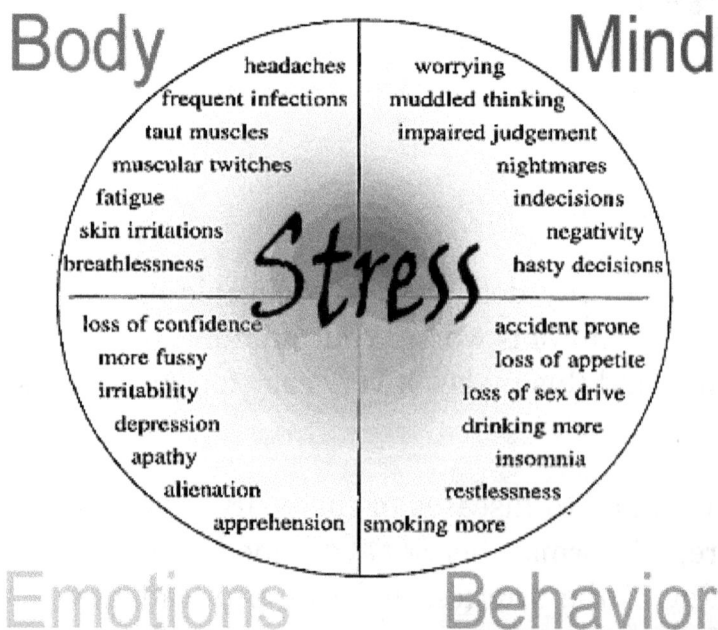

Body — headaches, frequent infections, taut muscles, muscular twitches, fatigue, skin irritations, breathlessness

Mind — worrying, muddled thinking, impaired judgement, nightmares, indecisions, negativity, hasty decisions

Emotions — loss of confidence, more fussy, irritability, depression, apathy, alienation, apprehension

Behavior — accident prone, loss of appetite, loss of sex drive, drinking more, insomnia, restlessness, smoking more

Stress

You may feel more tired and more irritable when you are stressed out. Your temper flares up more often, and even the slightest thing makes you jump out of your skin.

Studies have been done which show a direct link between stress and aggression. In fact, the two create a cycle: when we are under stress, our temper tends to flare; and when our temper flares, our stress increases.

Also, people who are dealing with stress often find that they start worrying more, even over the smallest things. It can be difficult to focus and stay on task, and you may start to feel as though things are just not worth doing any more.

As you can see, there is a broad range of symptoms or effects of stress. However, it is not necessary for all of these effects to be present to prove you are "stressed out."

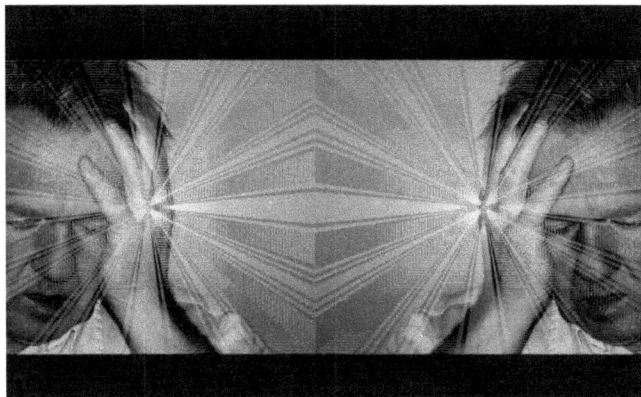

IDENTIFYING STRESSORS IN YOUR LIFE

There are thousands of people all over the world who spend a significant portion of their life doing things that the majority of us would consider extremely stressful and completely crazy! For example, some people will climb the tallest buildings or bridges or cliffs, strap a parachute to their back, and jump off. Certainly, there is stress in this situation. To the people who are involved in this or other "extreme" sports, the adrenaline rush that comes with the leap into the unknown makes the whole thing worthwhile and enjoyable.

Leaving aside the hobbies or activities that some people choose for entertainment which the majority of people would tend to avoid like the plague, it is still a fact that everyone gets stressed by completely different things. Some people will thrive in situations when the pressure is on, whereas others seem to fall to pieces in exactly the same scenario.

As an example, some high-powered individuals work best when under pressure with an unbreakable deadline that is looming ever larger, whereas other people would find such a situation intolerable. There are those who are excellent public speakers that are completely comfortable with standing up on a stage in front of thousands of people while many others would never dream of doing such a thing.

You get the picture, I'm sure. This list could go on, but the point is: what makes you stressed as an individual is likely to be completely different to the events or circumstances that will make your friends or even close family members feel stressed.

The important point is that you need to recognize the factors, events, and situations that are the primary causes of <u>your</u> stress. Only after you have done this can you begin addressing the effects of the stress in your life.

Some of your stressors may be obvious. For example, certain occupations – such as air traffic controller or firefighter – are naturally in a position where significant levels of stress are part of their everyday occupation. However, there may be other stressors that you don't realize are contributing to the levels of stress in your life.

photo by anna gutermuth, via flickr.com; creative commons license

Stress Less, Enjoy More

The American Psychological Association has been conducting an annual survey since 2007 examining the state of stress across the country. In addition to other results, the "Stress in America" survey identifies leading sources of stress.

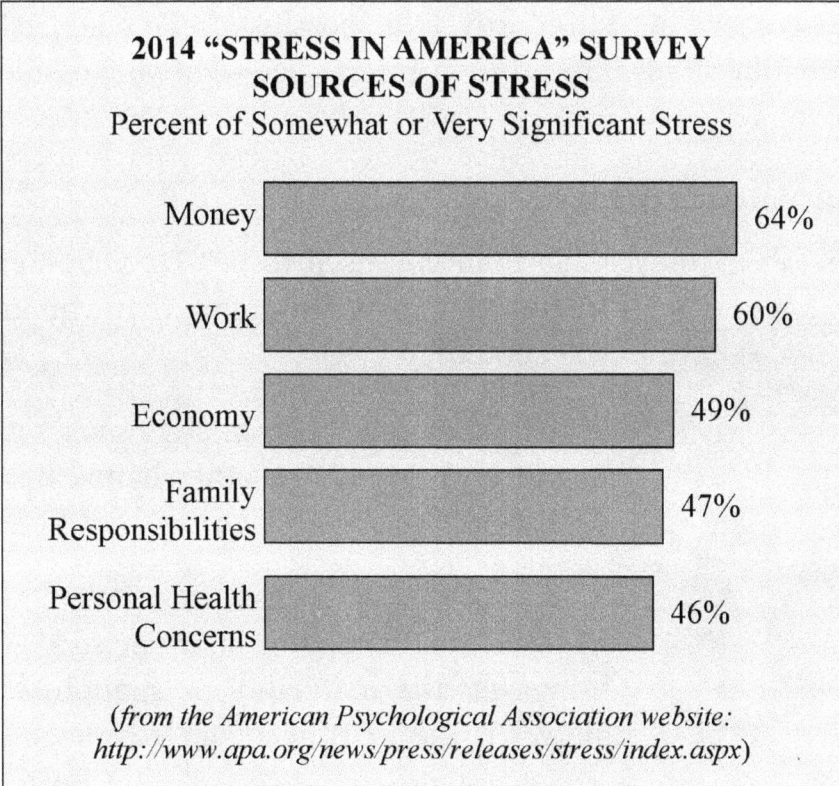

2014 "STRESS IN AMERICA" SURVEY SOURCES OF STRESS
Percent of Somewhat or Very Significant Stress

Source	Percent
Money	64%
Work	60%
Economy	49%
Family Responsibilities	47%
Personal Health Concerns	46%

(from the American Psychological Association website: http://www.apa.org/news/press/releases/stress/index.aspx)

In order to recognize the stressors in your life, you can go through a list of stressors to see which ones apply to you. There is a list in Appendix A if you want to do this. Another method is to look at some of the changes (stress indicators) that take place in your own life which could indicate a stressor. This may help you recognize things that were left off the list. There are four stress indicators to look for:

- Changes in the way you feel on an emotional level

- Bodily or physical changes

- Changes in the way that you are thinking
- Alterations in the way you are behaving physically

If you truly want to learn to "stress less and enjoy more" it is important to take some time from your busy schedule to assess your current life as objectively as possible. Let's take each of these four stress indicators in turn to see what you should be looking for.

Emotional Signs

Are you more irritable than you used to be? Do you snap at friends and loved ones more than you know you should?

Do you get angry far more quickly than previously? Or, on the other hand, are you persistently sad or worried?

If so, write down what causes you to be irritable and snappy or angry or sad. What brings on the irritability or snappiness or anger? These are triggers or stressors.

Physical Changes

Are you suffering far more aches and pains than you were six months or a year ago? Do you always feel tired and listless, without energy or enthusiasm for doing anything outside of your daily routine? How about headaches, dizziness or lightheadedness? All of these could be signs of stress, so try to analyze what you believe is causing these changes.

This may not be that easy to do as physical changes of this nature can often come on gradually or slowly. Because of this slow onset, there may not be any one event or situation that you can identify as being the starting point of your headache or backache problem, but you should be able to come up with an approximation of when you first noticed that you were suffering more aches and pains than previously.

If you can pinpoint the time when you first noticed that you seem to be suffering, so much the better; but if not, an approximation of when you first became aware of your problem is better than nothing. From this 'best guesstimate', you might be able to backtrack to assess whether there was something particularly stressful that might have caused it.

Different Thoughts

Do you find it harder to concentrate or remember things than you did in the past? It is a fact that, as we get older, all of us find that our memory is not as good as it used to be. However, if you can't concentrate and find it difficult to remember things, it could be indicative of a stress problem – particularly if you are still a relatively young person.

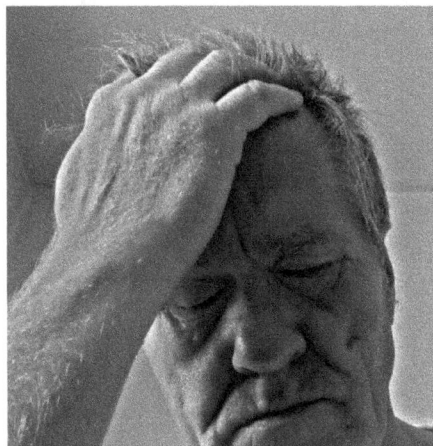

Again, try to identify when you first because aware of these changes so that you can then try to extrapolate whether there was any particular event or situation that caused it. This may not be that easy to do (I know: you can't remember!) but this kind of self-analysis is still critical and absolutely necessary.

Behavioral Changes

Have you started to drink a lot more than you used to or perhaps your 20 cigarettes a-day habit has now become a 40 a-day habit? Perhaps you've started using recreational drugs, or you find that you sleep too little or too much? The same might apply if you have started eating considerably more or considerably less than you used to consume.

All of these behavioral changes could be a reaction to stress, a way of escaping by indulging or denying yourself the right to indulge.

Create Your Stressor List

Once you have taken the time to go through this process, you will hopefully have a list of the factors that represent your own personal stressors.

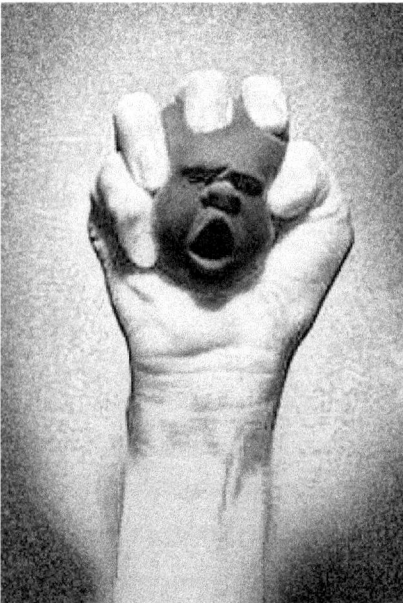

Go through your list and make a note of how often the stressor affects your stress level. Is it on a daily basis, weekly, or just once or twice a month? Make notes of how you react to each stressful situation. Do you get headaches, do you feel sick to your stomach, or do you start sweating profusely?

Next, you need to sort these stressors into some kind of priority list, with the factors or criteria that you think you are most susceptible to – those that cause you the most problems or upsets – at the top of your list.

Now you have a personal checklist of the stressors – the everyday situations or events – that seem to trigger your own personal stress reactions. Armed with this stressor list, you are ready to move on.

Before we talk about how to deal with the stress effects in your life, there is one more issue: do you have any "blocking" behaviors which increase the effect of stress in your life?

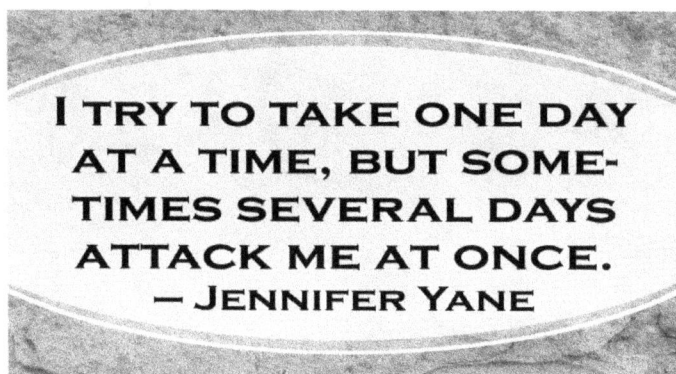

> **I TRY TO TAKE ONE DAY AT A TIME, BUT SOME-TIMES SEVERAL DAYS ATTACK ME AT ONCE.**
> **– JENNIFER YANE**

BEHAVIORS WHICH KEEP STRESS ALIVE

There are three "blocking" behaviors you may be engaging in that stop you from completely dealing with your stress. These behaviors can increase the effect of stressors on your life, and/or limit your ability to deal with the stress effects. Recognizing these behaviors in your life can be a great first step toward managing the problems that go with being too stressed.

Negativity

The first behavior which keeps stress alive is obsessive negativity. When you are obsessively negative, it means that you have a tendency toward being "negative" about people, places, situations, and things in your life.

A recent post on Facebook defined negative people as those who can find a problem for every solution!

Perhaps you find yourself saying things like "I can't do this!" or "No one understands!" or "Nothing ever works!" You may be doing this unconsciously, but this "sour grapes" attitude holds you back from enjoying the beauty in yourself and people around you.

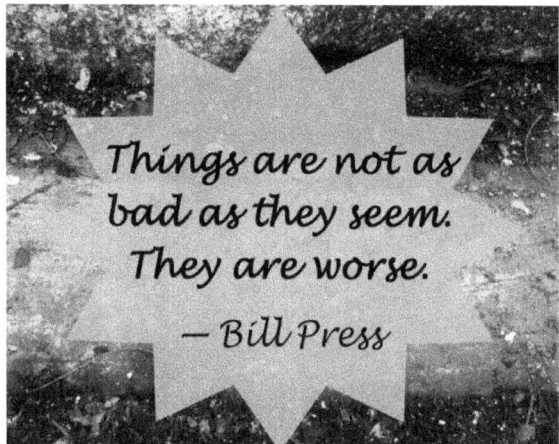

Things are not as bad as they seem. They are worse.

— Bill Press

Perfectionism

A second behavior which keeps stress alive is obsessive perfectionism. When you engage in obsessive perfectionism, you are centered on trying to do everything "just so" to the point of driving yourself into an anxious state of being. You may find yourself making statements such as, "I have to do this right, or I'll be a failure!" or "If I am not precise, people will be mad at me!" Again, you may not even be aware of this behavior in your life, but it greatly interferes with your ability to enjoy things without feeling "uptight" and "stressed."

Analysis

The final blocking behavior keeping stress alive is obsessive analysis. When you are obsessed about analyzing things, you find yourself wanting to re-hash a task or an issue over and over again. For instance, you might find yourself making statements such as, "I need to look at this again." Or "I need to study this and know it inside and out, or else I can't make a decision!" or "If I relax and let things go without looking them over repeatedly, things go wrong!"

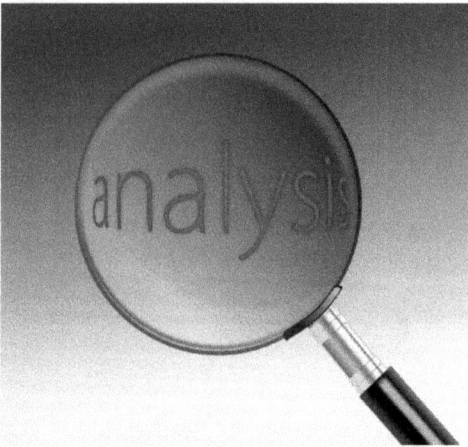

While analytical thinking is an excellent trait, if it's done in excess, you never get to stop and smell the roses. You're too busy trying to analyze everything and everyone around you. Gaining insight into this type of behavior is a major step toward letting go of stress.

> Stress is an ignorant state. It
> believes that everything is an
> emergency.
> — Natalie Goldberg, *Wild Mind*

Recognizing Blocking Behaviors

If you are unsure if you are engaging in any of the above "Blocking Behaviors", there are two things you can do to help yourself.

First, ask the people you know, love, and trust, "Am I negative about things?", "Do I complain a lot?", and "Am I difficult to be around?" This may be hard for you to listen to, as the truth sometimes hurts; but the insight you will get from others' assessment of you is invaluable. Accept their comments as helpful info, and know that you will gain amazing insights from what you hear.

Second, keep a journal to write down and establish patterns of when you are using "blocking behaviors." Even if you are not thrilled with the idea of writing, you can make little entries into a note book or journal each day. The great part is that you'll begin to see patterns in your behavior that reveal exactly what you're doing to prevent yourself from managing your stress.

We'll give you some great stress busting techniques beginning in the next chapter, but you need to recognize these blockages first so you can take the necessary steps to manage your stress.

PRACTICAL RESOURCES FOR MANAGING STRESS

As we already said, stress is a natural part of life. We cannot defeat stress; it is always going to be a part of life. Stress gives you a push to do your best in the various situations of your life. But, we still need to cope with the effects of stress – to learn to manage our reactions to the stressors – in order to reduce the negative effects and enjoy life.

If you go online or go to a bookstore and look up stress relief or stress management, you will find many articles and books telling you how to deal with your stress. While there may be some similarities, they will all have differences. This is because each person is unique, and there is not a single answer that works for all people.

It's important to learn to manage your stress levels by dealing with the triggers that cause your stress and with your reactions to the triggers in a way that minimizes the depth of your physical, emotional, behavioral, and mental reactions. So, in this book, you will find many techniques or tips to help you . . . but you have to find what works best for you.

This chapter includes eight techniques that are available to everyone. You may choose to use some or all of these; a combination is probably best. These eight "stress-busters" form the acronym T-R-A-N-Q-U-I-L since that is pretty much the opposite of stress!

T – Take Evasive Action

The first option for dealing with the stress triggers in your life is to take evasive action: remove yourself from any situation where you might suffer stress. If you can avoid stress in the first place, that takes care of the problem!

Of course, this simple solution may be relatively easy to do, or it may not – and it may be totally unrealistic. It is practically impossible to avoid stress these days. However, there are times when avoiding the stress is possible.

My doctor told me to avoid unnecessary stress, so I stopped going to doctors.
— Shira Tamir

One key to avoiding some stress triggers is to look at how you manage your time. It can be very helpful to prioritize the things you do on a regular basis. You may find there are things you can leave for the weekend or even delegate to another family member or to a work colleague.

You could have determined that the primary cause of your stress problem is a boss you hate. Therefore, you can easily get rid of your stress by quitting your job to go work elsewhere! ☺ However, this assumes there are other jobs available with better bosses. You could be jumping out of the frying pan and into the fire!

Just because it is not always practical or logical to avoid the stress triggers completely doesn't mean to ignore this as one possible solution. There are times when you will be able to remove the cause of your stress. You might be able to avoid people or places that get you stressed. You could be able to take a different route for your commute to avoid the worst traffic.

You need to review your list of stress triggers and determine if there are practical, reasonable ways to get rid of those triggers. If you can't avoid the triggers completely, you might still be able to decrease the amount of time that you involve yourself in that situation in order to decrease the stress.

Since most stressors tend to be a combination of things, this stress management technique definitely needs to be combined with others. Taking one action – such as quitting your job – is not going to give you all the solutions you need for managing your stress.

R – Rest/Relaxation

Getting plenty of rest is an essential stress-buster. Sleep as many hours as are needed to rest your body. Each of us has our own personal time clock. While most people need 6-7 hours of sleep (according to the experts), others need more.

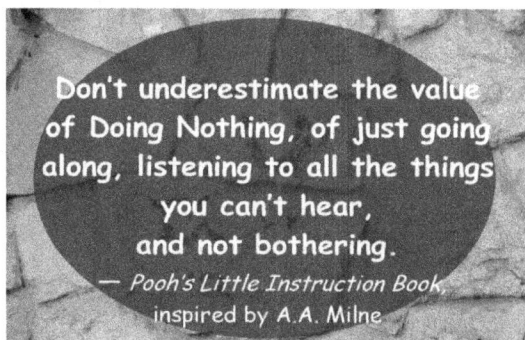

Don't underestimate the value of Doing Nothing, of just going along, listening to all the things you can't hear, and not bothering.
— *Pooh's Little Instruction Book,* inspired by A.A. Milne

Schedule restful vacations periodically. It may be a simple picnic in the park with a special friend. But, you really need to plan at least three hours per week when you can get away from responsibilities and recharge your batteries.

Find the things that help you relax. Some people relax by watching a movie, playing a game, listening to music, reading a good book, or even cooking. You have to identify what works for you.

Play with a dog or cat. This can be very relaxing. Experts say pet owners have longer lives and fewer stress symptoms than non-pet owners. Playing with your pet provides good vibrations – for you and your pet! It's a form of social interaction with no pressure to meet anyone's expectations.

Taking the time you need to rest/sleep and taking some time to relax can help you avoid getting stressed out. Appendix B describes a breathing and relaxation exercise which can be used anywhere – whenever you need to relax.

Meditation is used and advocated by many people as a way to rest and relax. Meditation is not an exotic, out-of-this-world technique that "weird" people practice. In most religions, a daily time of prayer is part of the recommended spiritual disciplines (this will be discussed more in the next chapter).

Whatever you use – whether prayer time, meditation, quiet time – it is a helpful tool which can give your mind a much-needed vacation – a rest – from the stress and pressure of daily life. This may range from 15-20 minute sessions up to hour-long sessions, but schedule a specific time each day when you can be quiet, without interruptions, and enjoy your solitude.

> For fast acting relief, try slowing down.
> — Lily Tomlin

In the Bible, we can see that God built rest in from the beginning. After six days of creation, God rested on the seventh day (Genesis 2:2). Then, in the Ten Commandments (and several other places throughout the Bible), we are told,

"Six days you shall labor and do all your work, but the seventh day is a Sabbath to the Lord your God. On it you shall not do any work, neither you, nor your son or daughter, nor your male or female servant, nor your animals, nor any foreigner residing in your towns." (Genesis 20:9-10)

This command is repeated numerous times throughout the Bible. God knows how vital it is for us to get rest!

Psalm 23 is a very familiar Bible passage to many people. It begins, *"The Lord is my Shepherd."* Even though I have read and heard this passage many times, I noticed something new recently. In a sermon earlier this year, Dr. Michael Wilson pointed out that verse 2 says, *"He makes me lie down . . ."* Makes me. I never noticed that before; it is so important for us to rest, that sometimes we need to be forced to lie down!

A – Altruism/Volunteering

Altruism/volunteering/helping others may not seem like an obvious management strategy for stress. However, helping others can also help you!

As you volunteer, you will take your mind off your own stress. Making a difference (for people, animals, or nature – your choice) will make you feel better about yourself and will improve your feelings of self-worth.

There are hundreds of volunteer opportunities. Some are short-term; others are on-going. You don't have to commit to a continuing volunteer job in order make a difference. There are even volunteer opportunities which you can do online from your own home.

If you don't know where to start, Volunteer Match (www.volunteermatch.org) is a site online which provides thousands of opportunities – some online. It will offer a list of many local options. You can also check with your church, your local United Way, or local Chamber of Commerce to find volunteer needs in your community.

Just don't fill your calendar to overflowing so the volunteering ends up adding to your stress!

N – Nutrition & Exercise

To deal with stress effectively, you have to take care of your body. Nutrition and exercise are two necessities.

This is not a diet book – there are thousands of those available. However, it is important to know that your stress level can be affected by food. Eating a healthy, balanced diet will help build up the immune system and lower blood pressure.

A simple diet is good. Some experts say a vegetarian diet is best to combat stress. While you may not choose to become a vegetarian, it is helpful to know that pastas, grains, and fresh fruits and vegetables have a calming effect on your system and do not aggravate the digestive tract.

Avoid fatty and over-processed foods as much as possible. Also, steer clear of things that contain a ton of sugar, such as soft drinks, cookies and fast foods. These can cause your blood sugar levels to spike. In turn this can mess up your body where one minute you are feeling great and the next you are tired and sluggish.

Avoid mindless eating. Eat when you're hungry, and don't overload your system in the evening hours.

Exercise is extremely important. Exercise will help you by releasing good endorphins which relieve the effects of stress.

Your regular exercise routine needs to be what works for you, and it will not be the same for everyone. You may choose a daily aerobics class, a brisk daily walk, or following along with a television exercise show.

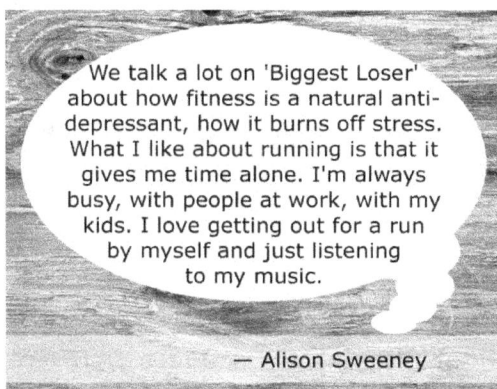

> We talk a lot on 'Biggest Loser' about how fitness is a natural anti-depressant, how it burns off stress. What I like about running is that it gives me time alone. I'm always busy, with people at work, with my kids. I love getting out for a run by myself and just listening to my music.
>
> — Alison Sweeney

The key is finding varied activities that are pleasing to your personality. Some people might thrive on high-impact exercise classes with lots of noise and music, while someone else might prefer strength training with weights. One person might choose a 20-30 minute walk around the block, and someone else will choose a ballroom dancing class. One person will choose yoga (an exercise that also includes relaxation techniques), and another will choose Tai Chi (an exercise which involves a series of slow, relaxed movements coordinated with deep breathing).

Q – Quality Relationships/Support System

An emotional support system is important for everyone. Everyone varies in their ability to be self-sufficient, but we all depend on others for certain things.

We need to recognize who is in our support system to help with psychological needs such as caring, understanding, and listening; and who can help with social needs such as belonging, group identity, and status. It may be the same people, or it may be different people. You may even need to expand your support systems.

Talking to someone, confiding in someone you trust, can really help. If doesn't mean you necessarily need their advice. Just letting it out and talking about your issues can be very good for you.

U – Unlock Your Inner Child

Give yourself permission to be a 'kid' again. What did you enjoy when you were a child? Draw; paint; be creative. Play with play-doh, dance, or read. Play music, allow yourself freedom to express yourself without worry that you're not keeping with the image of who you are "supposed" to be. Just relax and enjoy yourself. We all have a little child in us and it's a good idea to allow expression of the child within from time to time.

Swing. Remember the feeling of sitting in that little seat on the playground as you sway back and forth and feel the wind whipping through you hair? Do that! If you don't have a swing in your yard, go to a playground and remember to pump your legs back and forth to see how high you can go. It's liberating!

This stress management technique – to unlock your inner child – can be very therapeutic. You might find nothing is more satisfying than buying a brand new box of 64 crayons and coloring away in a coloring book. Your children and grandchildren will love seeing this!

Just let go. Run. Fly a kite. Play kickball. Giggle. Be silly. Unlock your inner child!

I – "It Doesn't Matter" Attitude

A "let go" or "it doesn't matter" attitude is very helpful. If you look around, you will find that those people who adopt a more relaxed, laid-back attitude to life tend to have fewer stress effects in their life.

When we get hung up on caring about all our worldly goods (house, TV, car, etc.), our focus gets narrowed to things that can be easily destroyed. We need to let go of our focus on acquiring things, let go of the agonizing over yesterday and worrying about tomorrow.

"No matter how much you stress or obsess about the past or future, you can't change either one. In the present is where your power lies."
— Mandy Hale,
The Single Woman: Life, Love, and a Dash of Sass

Be in the present. Don't continue to worry about something that happened in the past. That's over with. And don't worry about what's going to happen. It hasn't occurred yet. Living in the present moment means you aren't worrying about what has happened or what might happen.

Look at the big picture. How important will this situation be next week or next month? Will it matter in a year? Is it really worth getting stressed out about it? If not, then follow Elsa's advice in the movie *Frozen*, and "Let it go!"

Accept what is. We can't change everything or control everything. Those things shouldn't concern us. Don't worry about the things you can't change. Enjoy the moment of today.

> *"Therefore do not worry about tomorrow, for tomorrow will worry about itself. Each day has enough trouble of its own."*
> **(Matthew 6:34)**

L – Laughter

The last stress-buster in this chapter is laughter or humor. Humor helps us to cope with difficulties in several ways. For one, it draws our attention away from our upsets. By focusing our energy elsewhere, humor can diffuse our stressful events. It releases built-up tension and pops the cork off such things as fear, hostility, rage, and anger.

> A good laugh and a long sleep are the best cures in the doctor's book.
> — Irish Proverb

In 1979, editor Norman Cousins published his book *Anatomy of an Illness* in which he describes how he was diagnosed with a painful disease. He wondered "If negative thoughts can have negative physiological repercussions, can positive thoughts produce positive effects throughout the body?" In his book, he explains how he partly managed his illness by watching funny videos. He said that ten minutes of laughter gave him two hours of pain-free sleep during his recovery.

No matter if the stress is an embarrassing situation, a minor upset, or a major setback, if we can see some humor in it, we begin to disconnect and free ourselves from that event. Comedian Michael Pritchard equates laughter to changing a baby's diaper: "It doesn't change things permanently, but it makes everything okay for a while."

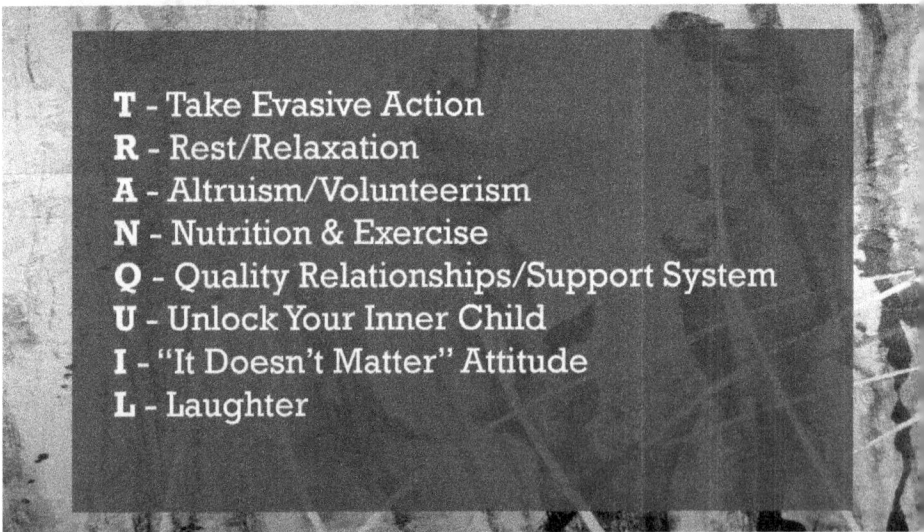

T - Take Evasive Action
R - Rest/Relaxation
A - Altruism/Volunteerism
N - Nutrition & Exercise
Q - Quality Relationships/Support System
U - Unlock Your Inner Child
I - "It Doesn't Matter" Attitude
L - Laughter

Appendix C has a "Coping Skills" test which you can take to see how well you are doing in using these practical techniques to help you manage your stress.

SPIRITUAL RESOURCES FOR MANAGING STRESS

The previous chapter included several techniques – which are available to everyone – for dealing with stress. In this chapter, we will talk about a few more techniques which are only available to those who are Christians – those who have accepted Jesus as Savior. (See Appendix D)

It is not religion, but a relationship with God through Jesus that makes a difference. With that relationship there are many promises of God's care for us. He will help us through life – through the stressors. Through Jesus, we can be overcomers!

In Matthew 11:28-29, we are told, *"Come to me, all you who are weary and burdened, and I will give you rest. Take My yoke upon you and learn from Me, for I am gentle and humble in heart, and you will find rest for your souls."*

This relationship with Jesus – and this rest – is offered to all. Read Appendix D to learn how to make this relationship with Jesus part of your life.

Through this book, I have tried to make it clear that stressors are everywhere, and <u>everyone</u> faces stress in their life. Believing in Jesus does not mean that we will have a stress-free life – look at Jesus Himself: In addition to the normal stresses of life, Jesus faced many other stressors:

- The people of His hometown *"drove Him out of the town, and took Him to the brow of the hill on which the town was built, in order to throw Him off the cliff"* (Luke 4:29)

- He was falsely accused of being *"demon-possessed"* Mark 3:22; John 7:20) and of being *"a glutton and a drunkard"* (Matthew 11:19)

- The religious leaders *"began to persecute Him"* (John 5:16) and *"they schemed to arrest Jesus secretly and kill Him"* (Matthew 26:4; Mark 14:1)

- One of His closest associates betrayed Jesus for money (Matthew 26:14-16; Mark 14:10-11; Luke 22:3-6; John 13:2)

- After His arrest, *"all the disciples deserted Him and fled"* (Matthew 26:56)

- *"Many false witnesses came forward"* (Matthew 26:60) so that Jesus was turned over to be put to death by crucifixion (according to historical accounts, crucifixion was a slow, painful, gruesome, & humiliating death)

- Even while dying on the cross, Jesus was mocked by people watching (Matthew 27:40-44; Luke 23:35-37)

These are just a few of the situations faced by Jesus which are listed in the Bible. Although Jesus' stressors were different from ours, it is obvious that His life was not trouble-free!

Just as Jesus faced stressors, Christians will, too . . . because we are not promised an easy, trouble-free life:

- *"In this world, you will have trouble"* (John 16:33)

- *"No temptation has overtaken you except what is common to mankind"* (I Corinthians 10:13)

- *"Dear friends, do not be surprised at the fiery ordeal that has come on you to test you, as though something strange were happening to you."* (I Peter 4:12)

The difference for Christians is that we do not have to deal with the stressors of life on our own. We have God in us, so we have access to the Comforter (the Holy Spirit).

In the last chapter, we used the acronym T-R-A-N-Q-U-I-L to describe the stress-busters available to everyone. In this chapter, we will use the acronym P-E-A-C-E. I chose this because of Jesus' own words: *"Peace I leave with you; My peace I give you. I do not give to you as the world gives. Do not let your hearts be troubled and do not be afraid."* (John 14:27)

> *"Come to me, all you who are weary and burdened, and I will give you rest. Take My yoke upon you and learn from Me, for I am gentle and humble in heart, and you will find rest for your souls."*
> Matthew 11:28-29

P – Pray

Prayer is just talking to God; it is not some difficult, mystical experience. Just as you talk with a friend, you can talk to God.

Most Christians seem to understand they can take their problems to God. However, the majority of people seem to think they should only take the BIG problems to God. But, Philippians 4:6-7 says, *"Do not be anxious about **anything**, but in **every** situation, by prayer and petition, with thanksgiving, present your requests to God. And the peace of God, which transcends all understanding, will guard your hearts and your minds in Christ Jesus."* (Emphasis added)

We sacrifice our chance for God's peace when we think we shouldn't bother God with the mundane, everyday things that cause us stress.

God loves us! If it bothers us, then God wants to help! God says that we should go to Him with **every** situation; **anything** that bothers us can be taken to Him.

> ### When we pray,
> ### God hears more than we say,
> ### Answers more than we ask,
> ### Gives more than we imagine . . .
> ### In His own time and
> ### His own way.

"In my distress I called to the Lord; I called out to my God. From His temple he heard my voice; my cry came to His ears." (2 Samuel 22:7)

When we pray and tell God about our concerns – our cares, our problems, our stresses – we are promised that He <u>will</u> sustain us. He will <u>never</u> let us go and will <u>never</u> fail us. *"Cast your cares on the LORD and He will sustain you; He will never let the righteous be shaken."* (Psalm 55:22)

Jesus is our example. We have already seen that He faced many troubles – many stressors – throughout His life. We are told of Jesus praying often:

- *"After He had dismissed them, He went up on a mountainside by Himself to pray."* (Matthew 14:23)

- *"Very early in the morning, while it was still dark, Jesus got up, left the house and went off to a solitary place, where He prayed."* (Mark 1:35)

- *"But Jesus often withdrew to lonely places and prayed."* (Luke 5:16)

- *"And being in anguish, He prayed more earnestly, and His sweat was like drops of blood falling to the ground."* (Luke 22:44)

- *"During the days of Jesus' life on earth, He offered up prayers and petitions with fervent cries and tears to*

the One who could save Him from death, and He was heard because of His reverent submission." (Hebrews 5:7)

Notice that the verse in Luke 5:16 says that Jesus <u>often</u> prayed. Good times, bad times, easy days, hard days – Jesus prayed.

Let's go back to the verse in Philippians 4:7. We are given a reassuring promise that taking our concerns to God will result in a peace that goes far beyond our understanding: *"And the peace of God, which transcends all understanding, will guard your hearts and your minds in Christ Jesus."*

E – Express Praise & Thanksgiving

In addition to praying, the verse in Philippians 4:6 says *"with thanksgiving."* In fact, it says we should present our prayers <u>with</u> thanksgiving. That means giving thanks is supposed to be part of the prayer – even before we have received an answer!

We can give thanks because of the promises that we have telling us that God always hears:

- *"God has surely listened and has heard my prayer."* (Psalm 66:19

- *"I love the Lord, for He heard my voice; He heard my cry for mercy."* (Psalm 116:1)

- *"This is the confidence we have in approaching God; that if we ask anything according to His will, He hears us."* (I John 5:14)

So, we can pray confidently and with thanksgiving, knowing that God always hears and answers. (This doesn't mean that God always answers the way we want, but He always answers with what is best for us and for His purposes.)

Praise and worship help us put things into perspective. Praising God puts our thoughts and focus on God; this takes our thoughts off ourselves and our problems. When we praise and worship, we are recognizing God for who He is. Our problems will seem small in comparison to our big God.

When we praise God and thank Him for the blessings He has given us already, it will give us the assurance that He is going to bless us this time as well. It will grow our faith which will increase our peace – thereby reducing the effects of stress!

A – Always Trust

Earlier we said that sometimes we don't want to "bother" God with our smaller problems. Well, the opposite is also true: we don't go to God with the big problems. Instead of trusting God, we focus on the problem or the stressors and become overwhelmed. We don't think we can trust God to handle it.

There is a book by J.B. Phillips called *Your God is Too Small*. Phillips said, "The trouble with many people today is that they have not found a God big enough for modern needs." Although the book was first published over 70 years ago, this statement is still true today.

Instead of our own mis-conceptions of God (i.e., we tend to create God in our own image, instead of seeing who He really is), we need to truly look at the God of the Bible. If we do that, we will be overwhelmed by God's awesomeness!

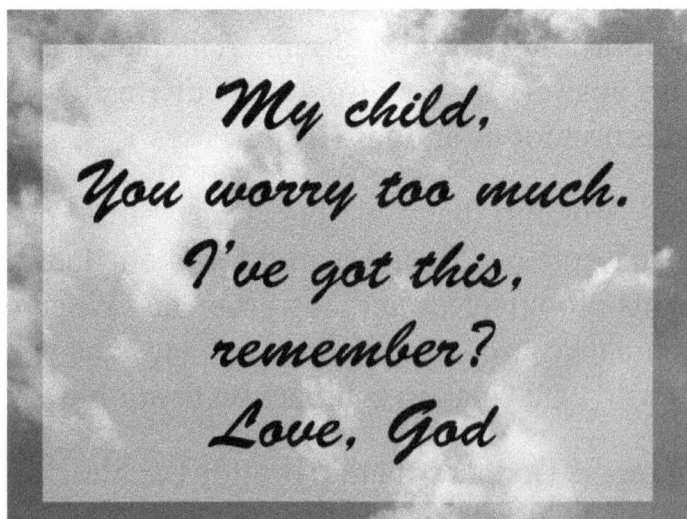

My child,
You worry too much.
I've got this,
remember?
Love, God

This awesome God is big enough to handle anything! All of our problems are smaller than God. We can trust Him to handle anything.

"You, dear children, are from God and have overcome them, because the One who is in you is greater than the one who is in the world." (I John 4:4)

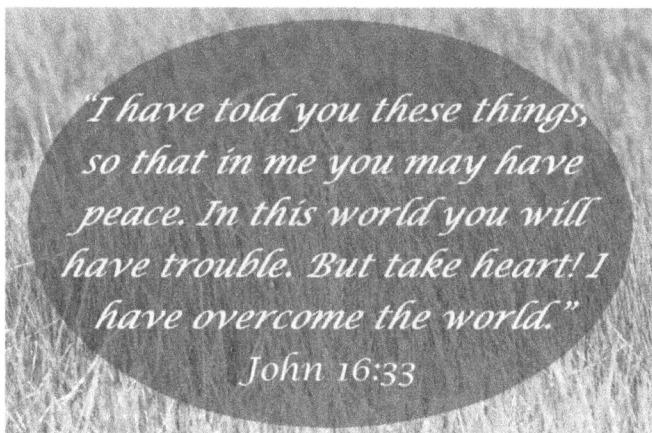

"I have told you these things, so that in me you may have peace. In this world you will have trouble. But take heart! I have overcome the world."
John 16:33

In the "Sermon on the Mount" in Matthew 6 and Luke 12, Jesus tells us over and over that we should not worry . . . that we can trust God:

- Matthew 6:25a & Luke 12:22a – *"Therefore I tell you, do not worry about your life"*

- Matthew 6:27 & Luke 12:25 – *"Can any one of you by worrying add a single hour to your life?"*

- Matthew 6:28 – *"Why do you worry about clothes?"*

- Matthew 6:31a – *"So do not worry, saying, 'What shall we eat?'"*

- Matthew 6:34a – *"Therefore do not worry about tomorrow, for tomorrow will worry about itself."*

- Luke 12:26 – *"Since you cannot do this very little thing, why do you worry about the rest?*

In most of these passages, Jesus is saying not to worry about the necessities of life. But, He also says not to worry about your life or adding hours to your life. In other passages, Jesus says not to worry about defending yourself before accusers – a big stressor!

- Matthew 10:19-20 – *"When they arrest you, do not worry about what to say or how to say it. At that time you will be given what to say, for it will not be you speaking, but the Spirit of your Father speaking through you."*

- Mark 13:11 – *"Whenever you are arrested and brought to trial, do not worry beforehand about what to say. Just say whatever is given you at the time, for it is not you speaking, but the Holy Spirit."*

- Luke 12:11-12 – *"When you are brought before synagogues, rulers and authorities, do not worry about how you will defend yourselves or what you will say, for the Holy Spirit will teach you at that time what you should say."*

Note that in each of these passages, Jesus tells us <u>why</u> we don't have to worry: because God will take care of it. We can trust Him.

"Trust in the LORD with all your heart and lean not on your own understanding; in all your ways submit to Him and He will make your paths straight." (Proverbs 3:5-6)

When we lean on our own understanding, we try to take care of things on our own, with our own strength. But, when we trust in the Lord with our whole heart, He will care for us.

We face so much stress because we do not always trust. This was true for the Israelites in Exodus 14 as they are beginning their escape from Egypt. In Exodus 14:10, it says *"they were terrified."* They thought they were going to die.

Exodus 14:31 says, *"And when the Israelites saw the mighty hand of the Lord displayed against the Egyptians, the people feared the Lord and put their trust in Him."* The Israelites waited until after they saw what God could do. If the Israelites had trusted God in the first place, they would have had His peace from the beginning.

We can always trust because God is always trustworthy. He will help us to face every situation, big or small. He is always there for us and always caring for us.

- *"Those who know your name trust in you, for you, Lord, have never forsaken those who seek You."* (Psalm 9:10)

- *"The Lord is my strength and my shield; my heart trusts in Him, and He helps me. My heart leaps for joy, and with my song I praise Him."* (Psalm 28:7)

- *"Surely God is my salvation; I will trust and not be afraid. The Lord, the Lord Himself, is my strength and my defense; He has become my salvation."* (Isaiah 12:2)

- *"So do not fear, for I am with you; do not be dismayed, for I am your God. I will strengthen you and help you; I will uphold you with My righteous right hand."* (Isaiah 41:10)

- *"The Lord is good, a refuge in times of trouble. He cares for those who trust in Him."* (Nahum 1:7)

- *"May the God of hope fill you with all joy and peace as you trust in Him, so that you may overflow with hope by the power of the Holy Spirit."* (Romans 15:13)

C – Contemplate/Meditate

When we talk about meditation, many people think of the eastern religions such as Buddhism. In this tradition, meditation seems to focus on thinking of nothing or having an "empty mind." This is NOT what we mean by meditation in this book.

The Merriam Webster Dictionary definition of the word meditation is "to focus one's thoughts on; reflect on or ponder over." In this case, it means the same thing as contemplate: "to think deeply or carefully about something."

Meditation is mentioned many times in the Bible. The meaning is always clear that meditation is focusing on God, focusing on His Word:

- *"Keep this Book of the Law always on your lips; meditate on it day and night, so that you may be careful to do everything written in it."* (Joshua 1:8)

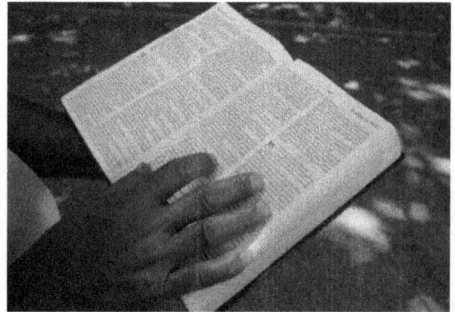

- *"Within Your temple, O God, we meditate on Your unfailing love."* (Psalm 48:9)

- *"I will consider all Your works and meditate on all Your mighty deeds."* (Psalm 77:12)

- *"I will meditate on Your precepts and consider Your ways."* (Psalm 119:15)

- *"My eyes stay open through the watches of the night, that I may meditate on Your promises."* (Psalm 119:148)

- *"They speak of the glorious splendor of Your majesty – and I will meditate on Your wonderful works."* (Psalm 145:5)

Notice the focus of the meditation/contemplation: God's word, God's love, God's deeds, God's ways, God's majesty, and God's wonderful works.

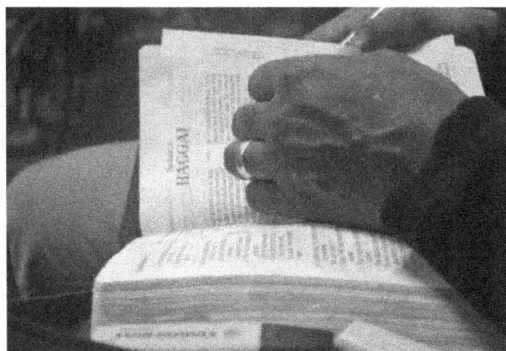

What do you contemplate during the day? Where do your thoughts dwell? Are you thinking about the terrible economy, the news stories of war and death, all the stuff on your to-do list, all the hassles and problems in your life? When your mind is focused on negative things, you get negative results: worry, fear, and more stress!

What happens when you meditate on God's Word and His promises to you? When your focus is the goodness of God, the results are peace:

- *"Great peace have those who love Your law, and nothing can make them stumble."* (Psalm 119:65)

- *"You will keep in perfect peace those whose minds are steadfast, because they trust in You."* (Isaiah 26:3)

- *"If only you had paid attention to My commands, your peace would have been like a river, your well-being like the waves of the sea."* (Isaiah 48:18)

- *"The mind governed by the flesh is death, but the mind governed by the Spirit is life and peace."* (Romans 8:6)

Focus, meditate, contemplate the positive, uplifting things of God. Think deeply about His goodness, His promises, His awesomeness. Pick one verse or passage that offers assurance to help dispel your stress, and read over it several times. Write it out. Let it fill your mind. As negative situations arise, take a minute to think of the verses. Let your mind dwell on the positive instead of letting the negative take over.

In the last section, the stress-buster was "always trust." If you use this stress-buster, "contemplate/meditate," you will find it easier to always trust!

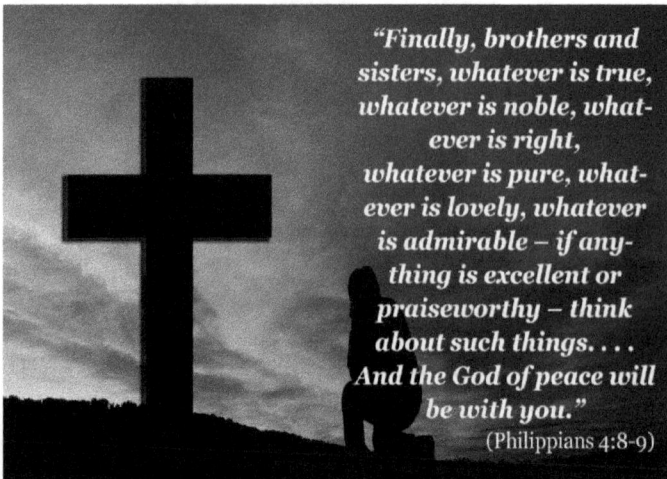

"Finally, brothers and sisters, whatever is true, whatever is noble, whatever is right, whatever is pure, whatever is lovely, whatever is admirable – if anything is excellent or praiseworthy – think about such things. . . . And the God of peace will be with you."
(Philippians 4:8-9)

E – Eternal Perspective

Throughout the Bible, there are stories of people who faced all kinds of trials (stresses) and got through them by focusing on the divine purpose – the end result.

Joseph was thrown into a well, then sold as a slave by his brothers. Later, he was put into prison after a false accusation. When his brothers (who had sold him into slavery) faced Joseph, Joseph's response was, *"You intended to harm me, but God intended it for good to accomplish what is now being done, the saving of many lives."* (Genesis 50:19) Joseph was able to focus on God's end result; Joseph was able to deal with all the things he faced because he kept an eternal perspective.

There are others, but the ultimate example is Jesus. Jesus faced rejection by the people around Him, the desertion of His followers, torture and mocking from the soldiers, and finally death on the cross.

Shortly before His arrest, Jesus said, *"My soul is overwhelmed with sorrow to the point of death."* (Mark 14:34) However, when Jesus prayed, He said, *"Now my soul is troubled, and what shall I say? 'Father, save me from this hour'? No, it was for this very reason I came to this hour."* (John 12:27)

Jesus had a clear sense of His purpose; He had an eternal perspective. Jesus did not allow the circumstances He was facing to take His vision off His eternal purpose.

> *"fixing our eyes on Jesus, the pioneer and perfecter of faith. For the joy set before Him He endured the cross, scorning its shame, and sat down at the right hand of the throne of God. Consider Him who endured such opposition from sinners, so that you will not grow weary and lose heart."*
> Hebrews 12:2-3

We have to keep an eternal perspective. Jesus knew the purpose of His crucifixion, so He was able to face the stresses and troubles in His life with peace. We may not know the reason for the trials and stresses in our life. But, we know God; and we know that He is in control. God is always working in our lives and will use every circumstance for our ultimate good.

> *"in all things God works for the good of those who love Him, who have been called according to His purpose."* (Romans 8:28)

- *"Dear friends, do not be surprised at the fiery ordeal that has come on you to test you, as though something strange were happening to you. But rejoice inasmuch as you participate in the sufferings of Christ, so that you may be overjoyed when his glory is revealed."* (I Peter 4:12-13)

- *"Consider it pure joy, my brothers and sisters, whenever you face trials of many kinds, because you know that the testing of your faith produces perseverance. Let perseverance finish its work so that you may be mature and complete, not lacking anything."* (James 1:2-4)

When we keep our eyes on Jesus and believe God is working in every situation, we can keep an eternal perspective. When we know there is a divine purpose for everything, it helps to diminish our stress!

Wrap-up for Spiritual Resources

We have said several times that stress is a natural part of life. We can't stop the stressors. But, we can determine how we will deal with the stress.

In the last chapter of "Practical Resources," we learned many stress-busters which can help. Those are all useful and can make a big difference. However, those are all focused on what we can do ourselves.

In this chapter, we have seen that Christians do not have to deal with stress on their own! When we believe in Jesus as our Savior, we have the Comforter living in our hearts. Through prayer, expressing praise and thanksgiving, always trusting, contemplating/meditating on God's Word and who He is, and keeping an eternal perspective, we will have the eternal resources of God's peace, joy, mercy, and grace.

P - Pray
E - Express Praise & Thanksgiving
A - Always Trust
C - Contemplate/Meditate
E - Eternal Perspective

CHILDREN AND STRESS

Children Are Affected by Stress

Stress does not only affect adults and seniors. Today, more and more children are developing signs of stress. There are many causes of stress for children including:

- Social pressures

- Being bullied

- Low self-esteem

- Lack of self-confidence

- Studying for exams

- Worrying about not fitting in

- Learning disabilities

- Physical disabilities

- Too busy of a schedule

- Not enough exercise

- Not eating correctly

- Being exposed to violence

- Physical or sexual abuse

- Alcohol/drugs

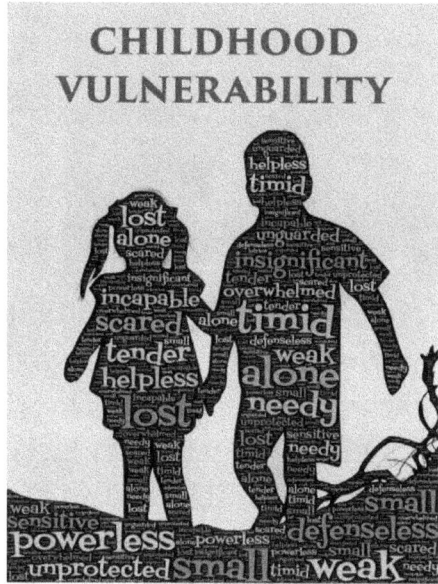

There really are more social pressures on your children today than ever before. They want and feel a need to fit in with the social crowd at school. They may feel pressured to look and dress a certain way.

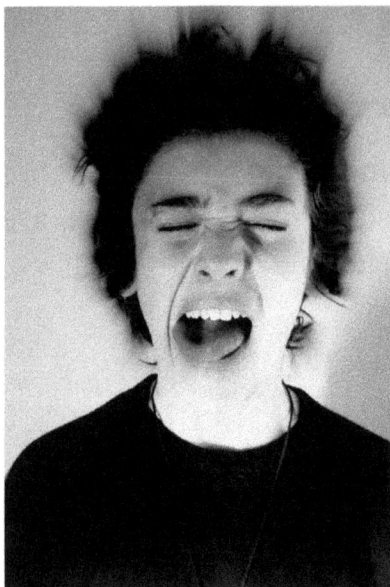

The stress for children can also be increased when they see their parents or other adults around them discussing all their troubles, or arguing about money, or worrying about the relative's illness, etc. Even the news can intensify the stress for children. When children see all the violence or disasters going on in the world, they may worry about the people around them or about their own safety.

Just as with adults, each child will react differently to stress. Those that have allergies and asthma may start having more attacks. They may overeat, or develop an eating disorder (such as bulimia or anorexia). The same effects which may be present for adults can also be present for children dealing with stress.

How a Parent/Concerned Adult Can Help

If you think your child may be dealing with too much stress, provide them with ways to cope with their stress. Just as with adults, children need to have plenty of sleep, healthy meals, and exercise.

The children may have too much on their schedule, and reducing their after-school activities is all that is required. As a parent, you may need to look at their schedules to see where it is overloaded. This includes the amount of homework and too many after-school activities.

Also, notice if there seems to be a lack of friends or a lack of social contact.

If your child is lacking in self-confidence or self-esteem try enrolling them in an activity such as martial arts or a self-defense program. This can help boost their confidence levels and in turn this can even help improve their grades at school.

Sometimes children are hiding extremely unhealthy stressful situations. Some children are committing suicide because they were bullied or raped and felt they had no one to turn to. While your child may not be willing or able to share his or her experience with you, provide them with access to someone who is capable of helping them deal with their stress.

Children may be stressed by things which seem minor to an adult. Don't dismiss the child's feelings; let them know that you understand they are feeling stressed. Help them know that feelings of anger, loneliness, or anxiety are normal. Support and reassurance are important.

It may be difficult to get your child to open up when you think they are dealing with stress. Make sure they know you are available to talk. They may not share immediately, but it could make them feel better just to know that you are there spending time with them.

Provide them with various outlets that can help them express their feelings such as:

- Giving them a personal journal

- Providing them with art material or some form of personal expression

- Getting them to write or draw out their feelings and include things such as if they are feeling happy, sad, lonely, and tired, etc.

In most cases, a parent will be able to help their child to deal with their stress. However, if you are concerned about your child's symptoms, or if their behavior is causing major problems at home or school, it may be time to seek professional assistance. Doctors or the counselors or teachers at school should be able to help you find resources for your child.

PROFESSIONAL HELP

This book is not a medical volume. We are providing you with some tools to implement in your life to help you better cope with those things that make you feel overwhelmed and out of control.

If the stress is too much for you to handle, don't be afraid to get professional help. Talk to your doctor, your pastor/spiritual advisor, or local mental health association about what is going on in your life and get suggestions on how to combat it.

Reactions to stress can be a factor in depression, anxiety, panic attacks, or other disorders; so it may be necessary to visit with a psychiatrist, psychologist, social worker, or other qualified counselor.

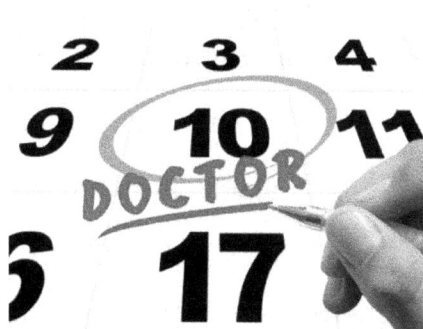

Anxiety and Stress Medications

Sometimes your doctor may recommend some pharmaceutical remedies. There are several different medications available for controlling anxiety and stress.

These pharmaceutical drugs often come with side effects that can be bothersome. The higher the dosage, the more noticeable the side effects become. These side effects can cause problems with work, school, or even everyday activities like driving. So, be sure to

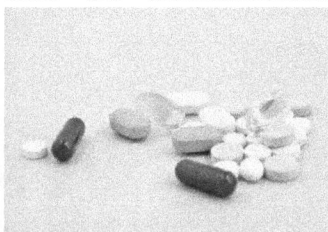

talk to the doctor about possible side effects so you know what you may be getting into.

Common side effects of anti-anxiety medicines include:

- Drowsiness, lack of energy
- Clumsiness, slow reflexes
- Slurred speech
- Confusion and disorientation
- Dizziness, lightheadedness
- Impaired thinking and judgment
- Memory loss, forgetfulness
- Nausea, stomach upset
- Blurred or double vision

Sometimes pharmaceutical medicines may be necessary to help you deal with the effects of stress in your life. Just be aware of the potential side effects each one can have.

CONCLUSION

If you've learned nothing else from reading this book, I hope you realize and understand that there is NO WAY to completely eliminate stress from your life. What you can do is to learn how to lessen or eliminate the effects of stress.

Stress is a normal part of life. In small quantities, stress is good -- it can motivate you and help you be more productive. However, too much stress, or a strong response to stress, is harmful.

It can set you up for general poor health as well as specific physical or psychological illnesses like infection, heart disease, or depression. Persistent and unrelenting stress often leads to anxiety and unhealthy behaviors like overeating and abuse of alcohol or drugs.

Just like causes of stress differ from person to person, what relieves stress is not the same for everyone. In order to deal with stress at its roots, you need to spend some time identifying what it is that causes you to be stressed. It may be one thing, but it is far more likely to be a combination of several situations or circumstances. You need to identify these factors to come up with your own triggers in order to tackle the problem head-on.

In general, making certain lifestyle changes as well as finding healthy, enjoyable ways to cope with stress helps most people. It will take some time and effort to make the changes in your life and in your reactions to stress.

In addition, those who are Christians – followers of Jesus – have additional stress-busters available to them. With the

Comforter (the Holy Spirit) living in our hearts, we will have the eternal resources of God's peace, joy, mercy, and grace.

Hopefully this book has given you some understanding of stress, stressors, the effects of stress, and – most importantly – some methods, techniques, and tips to help you manage your stress. You will have to work on the techniques and tips. It will not happen overnight. But, it can happen!

As I said in the introduction, thank you for reading this book. I hope you have gained many insights that will help you.

Now, you need to take action to manage your stress so you can **stress less and enjoy more!**

Feel free to connect with me on my website at:

http://www.PrepareForExcellence.com

Sherry M. Carroll

Appendix A – STRESSOR QUIZ

Go through the list and check which common pressures you have. Remember that a few small hassles add up and can be as stressful as one big event. There is no score for this quiz; however, it will help you recognize what stressors are affecting your life.

___ Death of a family member or friend

___ Divorce/separation

___ Child leaving home

___ Moving

___ Major change in health of yourself or a family member

___ Getting hurt or sick

___ Getting married

___ Having a baby

___ Changing jobs for yourself or spouse/partner

___ New responsibilities at work

___ Being fired

___ Being laid off from work

___ Retiring

___ Starting or ending school

___ High financial debt

___ Losing personal items through fire or theft

___ Legal problems

___ Frequent arguments with your spouse or partner

___ Sick or cranky kid

___ Not liking how you spend your day

___ Not liking your job

___ Problems at work

___ Problems with co-workers

___ Arguments or conflicts with in-laws or partner's family

___ Problems with your neighbors

___ Conflicts with friends

___ Friends letting you down or betraying your trust

___ Rejection by people you like

___ Too many things to do

___ Feeling overwhelmed by responsibilities

___ Setting high standards for yourself which are hard to meet

___ Having trouble meeting others' high standards of you

___ People taking you for granted

___ Being away from people you care about

___ Conflicts over money with family or friends

___ People taking advantage of you

___ Not enough time for fun and relaxation

___ Not enough time to take care of your responsibilities

___ Too many responsibilities and people who count on you

___ Not happy in your intimate relationship

___ Needing to make decisions about your intimate relationship

___ Being misunderstood by people in your life

___ Bad living conditions

___ No privacy

___ Being exposed to too much noise

___ Crowded home

___ New roommates

___ Being cheated

___ Feeling unattractive

___ Feeling unhealthy

___ People gossiping about you

___ Car problems

___ Home repairs

___ Traffic

___ Waiting in long lines

___ Running late for appointments

[From the U.S. Department of Health and Human Services and USA.gov.]

Appendix B – BREATHING & RELAXATION EXERCISE

Breathing and relaxation exercises can be used to:

- Achieve a state of calm
- Feel alive, invigorated, and ready for what you are facing
- Reduce stress in tense situations
- Wind down at the end of the day

When you wake up in the morning, you may wish to do the following exercise to feel invigorated and ready to go. When you're having a rough day at work or dealing with a conflict, you can use a few minutes to complete the exercise to help reduce stress. If you need a quick lift, you can take a few minutes and complete the exercise.

Whatever the reason, completing a breathing and relaxation exercise can provide several health benefits in addition to reducing stress:

- Reduce your blood pressure
- Calm your nerves
- Tighten your core muscles
- Aid in better digestion
- Aid in elimination of waste and toxins
- Bring you higher levels of energy
- Increase awareness of the functions within your body

Here is a basic, 5-10-minute exercise you can do at anywhere. Perform this exercise whenever you need to relax, whether it's on a plane or in a car or anyplace else you may be sitting.

Because this exercise may be very relaxing, <u>it should not be performed while driving.</u>

First and foremost, find a place to sit. Sit up straight with your back against the back of your chair, your feet flat on the floor, and your hands resting lightly on your thighs.

If possible, close your eyes. You may do the exercise without closing your eyes, but closing your eyes will help you relax a bit more. Do not clench your eyes shut. Let your eyelids fall naturally.

Breathe in slowly through your nose, counting to 5. Hold the breath for a count of 5. Breathe out slowly, counting to five. Repeat.

This exercise is performed by tensing and holding a set of muscles for a count of 5, and then relaxing the set of muscles for a count of 5.

When you tense each muscle set, do it as hard as you can without hurting yourself. When you release the hold, be as relaxed as possible.

Begin by tensing your feet. Do this by pulling the balls of your feet off the floor and your toes toward you while keeping your heels on the floor. Hold for a slow count of 5. Release the hold. Let your feet fall gently back. Feel the relaxation. Think about how it feels compared to when you tensed the muscles. Relax for a count of 5.

Next tense your thigh muscles as hard as you can. Hold for a count of 5. Relax the muscles and count to 5.

Tighten your abdominal muscles and hold for a count of 5. Relax the muscles for a count of 5. Be sure you are continuing to sit up straight.

Tense your arm and hand muscles by squeezing your hands into fists as hard as you can. Hold for a count of 5. Relax the muscles completely for a count of 5.

Tighten your upper back by pushing your shoulders back as if you are trying to touch your shoulder blades together. Hold for a count of 5. Relax for a count of 5.

Tense your shoulders by raising them toward your ears as if shrugging and holding for a count of 5. Relax for a count of 5.

Tighten your neck first by gently moving your head back (as if looking at the ceiling) and holding for 5. Relax for 5. Then gently drop your head forward and hold for 5. Relax for a count of 5.

Tighten your face muscles. First open your mouth wide and hold for 5. Relax for 5. Then raise your eye brows up high and hold for 5. Relax for 5. Finally clench your eyes tightly shut and hold for 5. Relax (with eyes gently closed) for 5.

Finish the exercise with breathing. Breathe in slowly through your nose, counting to 5. Hold the breath for a count of 5. Breathe out slowly, counting to five. Repeat 4 times. And that's it!

Over time, if performed regularly, this exercise will help you recognize tension in your body. You will be able to relax muscles at any time rather than performing the entire exercise. Perform at least twice a day for long-term results.

You may develop your own longer relaxation exercise by adding more muscle groups. Pinpoint your own areas of tension then tense and relax these areas in the same way.

Maximize the relaxation benefits of this exercise by visualizing a peaceful scene at the end of the exercise. Visualize a scene – a place where you feel relaxed – in detail for at least 5 minutes. Remember the happy place? Go there and enjoy it!

Appendix C – TEST YOUR COPING SKILLS

How do you cope with stress? There are many ways, but some are more effective than others.

This stress scale was created largely on the basis of results compiled by clinicians and researchers who tried to identify how people effectively cope with stress. It is an educational tool, designed to help inform you of the most effective and healthy ways to cope.

_____ Give yourself 10 points if you feel you have supportive family around you.

_____ Give yourself 10 points if you actively pursue a hobby.

_____ Give yourself 10 points if you belong to a social or activity group in which you participate more than once a month.

_____ Give yourself 15 points if you are within 10 pounds of your "ideal" body weight, considering your height and bone structure.

_____ Give yourself 15 points if you practice some form of "deep relaxation" at least five times a week. Deep relaxation includes meditation, progressive muscle relaxation, imagery and yoga.

_____ Give yourself 5 points for each time you exercise for 30 minutes or longer during an average week.

_____ Give yourself 5 points for each nutritionally balanced and wholesome meal you eat during an average day. A nutritionally balanced meal is low in fat and high in vegetables, fruits and whole-grain products.

_____ Give yourself 5 points if you do something you really enjoy and which is "just for you" during an average week.

_____ Give yourself 10 points if you have a place in your home to which you can go to relax or be by yourself.

_____ Give yourself 10 points if you practice time management techniques daily.

_____ Subtract 10 points for each pack of cigarettes you smoke during an average day.

_____ Subtract 5 points for each evening during an average week that you use any form of medication or chemical substance, including alcohol, to help you sleep.

_____ Subtract 10 points for each day during an average week that you consume any form of medication or chemical substance, including alcohol, to reduce anxiety or just to calm down.

_____ Subtract 5 points for each evening during an average week that you bring work home – work meant to be done at your place of employment.

Now calculate your total score. A "perfect" score is 115. If you scored in the 50-60 range, you probably have adequate coping skills for most common stress. However, keep in mind that the higher your score, the greater your ability to cope with stress in an effective, healthy manner.

This stress assessment was created by Dr. George Everly Jr. of the University of Maryland. It is reprinted from a U.S. Public Health Service pamphlet, "What Do You Know About Stress" (DHHS Publication No. PHS79-50097) and is in the public domain.

Appendix D – SPIRITUAL LIFE

I am a Christian. I believe the Bible, I pray, I fellowship with other believers, and I am active in my local church. I know that not all of the readers of this book believe the same, and that is your choice. However, my desire is that all of you will have Christ live in your hearts by faith, and that you will come to know and understand how wide and long and high and deep is the love of Christ, and that you will know this love that surpasses all knowledge, so that you may be filled with the fullness of God (from Ephesians 3:18-19).

The gospel (this just means "the good news") is available to everyone. Here is what you need to know (adapted from the nambmit.publishpath.com website.]

What is the Most Important Thing?

When we ask that question, we receive many different answers. What would be your answer? Was it the day you got the job you have now? Your wedding day? The day your kids were born?

I will tell you that the most important thing that can happen to you is a result of the most important thing God has ever done for you. **God loves you** and He showed you how much through the cross.

The word C-R-O-S-S will help you discover how you can experience the most important thing: eternal life. You can know God loves you because of the cross.

C – Christ Jesus

Christ Jesus, the Son of God, died on the cross.

The Bible says, *"But God demonstrates His own love for us; while we were still sinners, Christ died for us."* (Romans 5:8)

There are three things we need to know about Christ Jesus:

1. The Bible teaches that Jesus is God. Jesus forgave sins, healed the sick, raised the dead, received worship; and after He died on the cross, He rose again just as He promised.

2. Jesus was sinless. The angel Gabriel told Mary that the Holy One to be born would be called the Son of God. On one occasion, Jesus asked the religious leaders if they could prove Him guilty of sin. They could not. Jesus was sinless all the days of His life.

3. Jesus died on the cross.

R – Reason

Why did Jesus die on the Cross? The reason Christ died is for sin.

The simplest explanation of sin: sin is our failure to measure up to God's holiness and His righteous standards. We sin by the things we do, the choices we make, and the attitudes we show. We also sin when we fail to do right things. No matter how good we try to be, none of us does the right thing all the time.

"For Christ died for sins once for all, the righteous (that was Jesus) *for the unrighteous* (that was us) *to bring you to God."* (I Peter 3:18a)

The Bible, our conscience, and the Law of God testify we have fallen short of God's standard. All are guilty before God.

"For all have sinned and fall short of the glory of God." (Romans 3:23)

O – Outcome

The outcome of sin is death.

The Bible says, *"For the wages of sin is death"* (Romans 6:23a)

Wages are what we earn or deserve. If someone hired you to work one day for $100; at the end of the day, he would owe you $100. That is what you earned, what you deserve. The outcome or wages of our sin is death. This is bad news.

Despite the fact that we are all sinners, there is wonderful news: **God loves us**. He loves me, and He loves you! God loves us so much that He made a way for us to become His children – not because of anything you can do for Him – because **GOD LOVES YOU**. And, this brings us to the first S in CROSS.

S – Substitute

Jesus was our substitute on the cross. Jesus' sacrifice displays God's loving mercy and His righteous justice as no other action could.

"God made Him who had no sin to be sin for us, so that in Him we might become the righteousness of God." (2 Corinthians 5:21)

Jesus paid the sin-debt that we could not pay. God then raised Him from the dead to demonstrate that the debt was paid and that Jesus is exalted as Lord over all.

Suppose you received your credit card bill, and it was so large you could not pay it. Suppose your creditors took you to court and the judge found you guilty and sentenced you to prison until the debt was paid. How is the debt going to be paid while you sit in jail? Then, just when all seems hopeless, a stranger walks up and asks the judge if he could pay your debt. The judge lets him pay and you go free. How would you feel about this person who paid your debt?

When Christ became the substitute for sin, He satisfied the righteousness and justice of God and demonstrated the love and mercy of God. Christ's resurrection displays the power of His Lordship, Jesus offers what He has done as a gift from God. This gift, like any gift, must be received. That brings us to the last S in CROSS.

S – Salvation

Because Jesus is our substitute, He is the only One who can offer salvation. Salvation includes forgiveness of sin and the gift of eternal life. But how is this possible?

To have forgiveness and eternal life, you must believe and receive.

- <u>To believe</u>, the Bible says, *"That if you confess with your mouth, that 'Jesus is Lord,' and believe in your heart that God raised Him from the dead, you will be saved."* (Romans 10:9). To confess Jesus as Lord means you turn from sin (repent) and surrender control of your life to Jesus. To believe in your heart that God raised Him from the dead means you are trusting in all that Jesus Christ is and has done for you.

- To receive Christ by faith is simply trusting Christ Jesus alone for salvation. The Bible says, ". . . *to all who received Him, to those who believed in His name, He gave the right to become children of God.*" (John 1:12)

Here is a simple prayer you can use to make the decision for yourself (or you can use your own words):

Dear God, I know I am a sinner. I believe Christ Jesus died on the cross for my sin and then arose. I now turn from my sin and confess You as Lord and trust You alone for my salvation. I believe You and receive You by faith. Thank You for the free gift of eternal life. Amen.

If you just prayed that prayer for the first time and have trusted Jesus as your Savior, you need to tell someone! I would love to hear about it, so I can rejoice in what God has done in your life.

Here is contact information for the North American Mission Board, "Most Important Thing" website contact form. They will gladly help you understand the love of Jesus, will answer any questions or concerns you would like help with, and will help you find a local gathering where you can study the Bible and grow spiritually:

http://nambmit.publishpath.com/response-form

If you want to go through this information again, the website provides some video going through "The Most Important Thing" beginning at: http://nambmit.publishpath.com/video.

AUTHOR'S PAGE

I have worked in social services and ministry throughout my professional career. I have been executive director of three different non-profits (one was a ministry); served as a missionary for 2 years in Zambia before getting married; served as a missionary in South Korea for 7 years with my husband; have been active in Girl Scouts, Red Cross, Chamber of Commerce, Special Olympics, and other service organizations; and have always been active in my local church (including as a pastor's wife!).

My focus with books is to guide people to incorporate values and character into every aspect of life – work, home, and play – leading to personal fulfillment and success.

My website: http://PrepareForExcellence.com offers information and inspiration on various areas of personal development, as well as details of the first book in the "Prepare for Excellence" series: *Mindset of a Winner: The Character Traits Necessary for a Life of Success – a Life of Excellence.* Here is a link to the book:
(http://truthfamilylikes.com/mindset)

Being a Christian is not something that only happens on Sunday – it is an essential part of my life, and I believe it should permeate everything I do. Therefore, my personal development books include Biblical principles in addition to other material.

I hope you find the books useful, practical, and uplifting!

Sherry M. Carroll

www.ingramcontent.com/pod-product-compliance
Lightning Source LLC
Chambersburg PA
CBHW071836020426
42331CB00007B/1745